The Gate Theatre presents

THE PROPHET
HASSAN ABDULRAZZAK

Premiered in the UK at the Gate Theatre, Notting Hill
on 14 June 2012

Supported using public funding by
**ARTS COUNCIL
ENGLAND**

THE PROPHET
HASSAN ABDULRAZZAK

Cast (in alphabetical order)

Layla | **Sasha Behar**

Hani / Metwali | **Silas Carson**

Suzanne | **Melanie Jessop**

Hisham | **Nitzan Sharron**

Creative Team

Director | **Christopher Haydon**

Design | **Holly Pigott**

Lighting | **Mark Howland**

Music & Sound | **Alex Baranowski**

Video & Projection | **Dick Straker**

Assistant Director | **Jude Christian**

Associate Lighting | **Joshua Pharo**

Costume Supervisor | **Lydia Hardiman**

Scenic Artist | **Jemima Robinson**

Voice Coach | **John Tucker**

Fight Director | **Terry King**

Production Manager | **Bernd Fauler**

Company Stage Manager | **Kate Schofield**

Deputy Stage Manager | **Rachael Miller**

Press | **Kate Morley**

for DDA Blueprint (kate@ddablueprint.com | 07970 465648)

Photographer | **Simon Kane**

THE PROPHET is part of the RESIST! Season,
which is supported by Jenny Hall

Cover Image © George Henton www.negativespace.asia

SUBSIDISED REHEARSAL FACILITIES PROVIDED BY

JERWOOD **SPACE**

Hassan Abdulrazzak – Writer
Previous theatre credits include: *Baghdad Wedding* (Soho; winner of the George Devine, Meyer-Whitworth and Pearson awards). Previous translations include: *603* by Imad Farajin; *Voluntary Work* by Laila Soliman (Royal Court).

Alex Baranowski – Music & Sound
Alex Baranowski is a graduate of Paul McCartney's LIPA. Theatre credits include *Hamlet* (National); *Earthquakes in London* (Headlong / National); *Frankenstein* (National, as Music Associate with Underworld - nominated 2012 Olivier Award for best Sound Design). Also *Salt, Root and Roe* (Donmar Trafalgar, nominated 2012 Olivier for Outstanding Achievement in an Affiliate Theatre); *Betrayal, Othello* (Sheffield Crucible); *The Faith Machine* (Royal Court); *The Merchant of Venice* (RSC – with Adam Cork); *Sea Plays* (Old Vic Tunnels). Music for dance includes *Ballet Black* (Royal Opera House). Music for film includes *McCullin, Made in England, Future.Inc, I Won't Go*. www.alexbaranowski.co.uk

Sasha Behar – Layla
Sasha studied Classics at Cambridge University and trained at The Poor School. Theatre credits include: *The Bitter Tears of Petra Von Kant* (Southwark); *The Strange Wife - A Response to Ezra* (Bush); *Macbeth* (Leicester Haymarket); *Troilus and Cressida* (Oxford Stage Company); *The Trackers of Oxyrhnchus* (West Yorkshire Playhouse); *Paper Husband* (Hampstead). Sasha has worked extensively at the RSC, credits include: *The Island Princess, Eastward Ho, The Malcontent, Les Enfants Du Paradis, Son of Man, Pentecost*. Television credits include: *Sherlock - Hound of the Baskervilles, Strikeback II, Injustice, The Shadow Line, New Tricks, Jonathan Creek, Messiah V, Dr Who IV, Lewis, Poirot, Rescue Me, North Square*.

Silas Carson – Hani / Metwali
Previous credits for the Gate include: *Shakuntala*. Other theatre credits include: *The Comedy Of Errors* (National); *Ruined, Macbeth* (Almeida); *Arabian Nights* (RSC); *Much Ado About Nothing* (Regent's Park); *Baghdad Wedding* (Soho); *Homebody/Kabul* (Cheek By Jowl); *A View From The Bridge* (Sheffield Crucible); *A Doll's House* (Young Vic); *Dracula* (BAC); *Romeo And Juliet* (Lyric Hammersmith); *Unidentified Human Remains* (Traverse). Film credits include: *Clean Skin, Pimp, Boogie Woogie, Franklyn, Flawless, Chromophobia, Hidalgo, Star Wars Trilogy*. TV credits include: *Strikeback II, Holby City, How Not To Live Your Life, Hunter, Bonekickers, Waterloo Road, Outnumbered, The IT Crowd, Hustle, Spooks, Absolute Power, The Grid*.

Jude Christian – Assistant Director

Jude trained on the MA Directing Course at RADA. Directing credits include: *ConcertTheatre – Sonata Movements* (Blue Elephant Theatre); *My Romantic History* (English Theatre Berlin); *Love and Money* (London Business School); *Last Easter* (GBS Studio); *Stand and Deliver, City of Angels* (Aylesbury Vale Youth Theatre). Assistant/trainee directing includes: *On the Twentieth Century* (Union Theatre); *Ein Mädchen namens Elvis* (Deutsches Theater); *Company* (RADA). Musical directing/composing credits include: *Skunk, In Search of Obama* (National Youth Theatre); *Breathe* (Battle for the Winds, 2012 Olympics, Weymouth Beach). Jude is a senior associate of Diverse City, artistic director of AT ConcertTheatre and a Creative Associate at the Gate.

Bernd Fauler – Production Manager

Theatre credits include: *Krapp's Last Tape/Spoonface Steinberg, Once Upon A Time In Wigan* (Hull Truck Theatre); *The Roundabout Season Sheffield – One Day When We Were Young, Lungs & The Sound Of Heavy Rain; 65 Miles; WASTED; A Play A Pie And A Pint* (Paines Plough); *Trashing Performance & Access All Areas* (Live Art Development Agency); *London via Lagos Season* (Oval House Theatre); *SACRED '09 & '10, A season of contemporary performance* (Chelsea Theatre); *Howard Barker Season: Hurts Given & Received / Slowly* (Riverside Studios); *Krunch* (Talawa Theatre Company).

Lydia Hardiman – Costume Supervisor

Lydia works as a costume designer and supervisor for theatre, film and dance. As costume supervisor she has worked with the Queen's Theatre Hornchurch, Margate Theatre Royal, Regent's Park Open Air Theatre, Glitter Pantomimes, Frantic Assembly, Told By An Idiot and 30 Bird Productions. Recent theatre design credits include: *Drumchasers* (National Tour); *Oliver, The Lion The Witch and the Wardrobe, The Adventures of Mr Toad* (Gordon Craig Theatre); *Circus?, Guys and Dolls, Into the Woods* (Urdang Academy). Most recently Lydia's designs were worn by the 4 Corners dance troupe for their appearance in the semi-finals of Britain's Got Talent.

Christopher Haydon – Director

Christopher is the Artistic Director of the Gate Theatre. He studied at Cambridge University, the Central School of Speech and Drama, and the National Theatre Studio. In 2007 he received both the inaugural Chichester Festival Theatre Heller Fellowship and the Channel Four Theatre Director's Bursary at the Salisbury Playhouse. He is the Associate Director of On Theatre and formerly an Associate Director at the Bush Theatre. Credits for the Gate include: *Wittenberg*. Other theatre credits include: *Sixty Six Books, In The Beginning* (Bush Theatre/ Westminster Abbey); *A Safe Harbour for Elizabeth Bishop* (Southbank

Centre); *Pressure Drop* starring Billy Bragg and his band (Wellcome Collection); *Deep Cut* (Sherman Cymru/National Tour); *Monsters* (Arcola Theatre); *A Number* (Salisbury Playhouse); *Grace* (British Council/On Theatre, Theatre Du Poche, Brussels, Belgium); *Notes from Underground* (Arcola Theatre). He is also an award winning journalist and has written for *The Financial Times, The Scotsman, Prospect Magazine, The Guardian* and *The New Statesman.* He has coedited several books including: *Conversations on Truth, Conversations on Religion* (both published by Continuum) and *Identity and Identification* (published by Black Dog/ Wellcome Collection).

Mark Howland – Lighting

Mark studied, briefly, at Oxford University prior to training in Stage Lighting Design at RADA. Credits for the Gate include: *The Kreutzer Sonata* (2012 revival), *Yerma, Wittenberg, The Kreutzer Sonata* (2009), *Vanya.* Other credits include: *Canvas* (Chichester Festival), *Ghosts, Sweeney Todd* (Aarhus Theatre, Denmark); *Singin in the Rain* (New Theatre, Copenhagen), *One Flew Over the Cuckoo's Nest, Absurd Person Singular, Molly Sweeney, Translations* (Curve); *Measure for Measure* (Sherman Cymru); *Bea, Pressure Drop, On Religion* (On Theatre); *Six Dance Lessons in Six Weeks* (Vienna's English Theatre); *Dick Turpin's Last Ride, Much Ado About Nothing, Cider with Rosie, The Merchant of Venice* (Theatre Royal Bury St Edmunds); *Uncle Vanya, Dockers, The Home Place* (Lyric Theatre, Belfast); *A Number* (Salisbury Playhouse); *Topless Mum* (Tobacco Factory); *Monsters* (Arcola Theatre); *The Pains of Youth* (Belgrade Theatre).

Melanie Jessop – Suzanne

Theatre includes: *Single Spies* (Watermill); *Taking Sides* CFT/West End); *What the Butler Saw* (Salisbury); *King Lear, The Seagull* (RSC Stratford, World Tour and West End); *The Duchess of Malfi* (West Yorkshire Playhouse); *Romeo and Juliet* (Shakespeare's Globe); *Scenes from an Execution* (Hackney Empire); *David Copperfield* (Greenwich/Sheffield Crucible); *The Prisoner of Zenda* (Greenwich). TV includes: *Poirot, A Touch of Frost, Absolutely Fabulous.* Melanie is an Associate of The Wrestling School and has worked extensively for the company, and with Howard Barker. Her work for the company includes: *Victory, Ego in Arcadia, Judith, Und* (which was written for her) and *Blok/Eko.*

Rachael Miller – Deputy Stage Manager

Theatre credits include: *Anne Boleyn* (English Touring Theatre, Shakespeare's Globe); *Beauty and the Beast* (Jordan Productions); *66 Books* (Bush Theatre); *Eden End* (English Touring Theatre, Royal & Derngate); *Yes, Prime Minister* (Gielgud Theatre, Chichester Festival

Theatre); *The Firebird, The Rise and Fall of Little Voice, A Christmas Carol, The Elephant Man, The Cherry Orchard, Balgay Hill, Sunshine on Leith* (Dundee Rep Theatre).

Joshua Pharo – Associate Lighting

Joshua is a graduate of Rose Bruford College of Theatre and Performance, majoring in Lighting Design. Previous credits for the Gate include: *The Kreutzer Sonata* (also at La MaMa in New York). Other previous lighting credits include: *Purge* (Borealis Theatre Co, Arcola Theatre); *Do We Look Like Refugees?!* (NT Studio, Riverside Studios, The Drum, Plymouth); *Cracking-After Medea* (Iso Theatre Co, Wimbledon Studio); *Saint Saviour* (Bush Hall, Channel 4, Hoxton Hall, XOYO, Somerset House). Credits as Associate Lighting Designer include: *The Infant, The Vaudevillians* (Les Enfants Terribles, Charing Cross Theatre, Lowry Manchester, UK Tour). www.joshuapharo.co.uk

Holly Pigott – Design

Holly graduated from the Royal Welsh College of Music and Drama in 2011 with a First Class Honours in Theatre and Performance Design. Since finishing she was shortlisted as one of 12 finalists in the Linbury Prize for Stage Design, where she worked with ROH2 on a conceptual design for *OperaShots* in the Linbury Studio. Her work on this project was exhibited at the National Theatre in November 2011. From July, she will be working with the Royal Shakespeare Company as an Assistant Designer where she plans to continue her development in the industry. Previous design credits include: *Sex With A Stranger* (Trafalgar Studios); *Who's Afraid Of Rachel Roberts* (Torch Theatre tour); *Hitchcock Blonde* (Chapter Arts Centre, Cardiff). Previous assisting credits include: *A Provincial Life* (Sherman Theatre, Cardiff); *The Passion* (Port Talbot); *Cappuccino Girls* (New Evening Post Theatre, Swansea). Holly is one of the Gate's Jerwood Young Designers for 2012.

Jemima Robinson – Scenic Artist

Jemima was a winner of the biennial Linbury Prize for Stage Design in 2011. Design credits include: *Love's Labour's Lost* (Circomedia); *The Aliens* (Alma Tavern & Trafalgar Studios); *Pride and Prejudice* (Bristol Old Vic Studio); *Ignite 6* (Old Vic Tunnels); *My previous self* (Wardrobe Theatre); *Finer Noble Gases and Lobby Hero* (Masterclass – Theatre Royal Haymarket). Previous assisting credits include: *The Two Worlds of Charlie F* (Theatre Royal Haymarket); *House of Cards* (Kensington Palace). Forthcoming designs include: *New English Ballet Theatre* (Sadlers Wells); *The Tempest* (Watermill Theatre, Newbury). www.jemimarobinson.com

Kate Schofield – Company Stage Manager
Previous credits for the Gate include: *The Measles, Franziska, Herakles.*
Other theatre credits include: *Missing* (Gecko at Dance East, Ipswich);
His Teeth (Only Connect); *Cinderella* (The Lighthouse Theatre); *The Comedy of Errors, The Importance of Being Earnest* (Oxford Shakespeare Company & regional outdoor tour); *Blackbirds* (London Bubble - Dilston Grove); *The Sirens of Titan* (London Bubble - outdoor tour); *The Southwark Mysteries* (Southwark Cathedral); *Anansi: An African Fairytale* (Southwark Playhouse).

Nitzan Sharron – Hisham
Previous theatre credits include: *A View From The Bridge* (Royal Exchange); *Salome* (Hampstead & Tour); *Mad Forest, A Thought In Three Parts* (BAC); *The White Devil* (Menier); *Romeo and Juliet* (Shakespeare's Globe & Tour); *Baghdad Wedding* (Soho); *Two Thousand Years* (MEN nominated), *Sparkleshark* (National); *Chicken Soup with Barley, Ritual in Blood* (Nottingham Playhouse); *Henry IV* (Donmar); *CrazyBlackMotherFuckin'Self, Bazaar* (Royal Court); *The Jew of Malta* (Almeida); *Cause Celebre* (Lyric Hammersmith); *The Day The Bronx Died* (Tricycle); *Shadowlands* (Queens Theatre). Film credits include: *The Debt, The Gospel According to St John, Devil's Arithmetic, Simon Magus, Christopher Columbus: The Discovery.* Television credits include: *Mister Eleven, Nuclear Race, Holby, The Bill, Daniel Deronda, McCallum, Broken Glass, Dangerfield, Grange Hill.*

Dick Straker – Video & Projection
Theatre credits include *A Marvellous Year For Plums* (Chichester Festival Theatre); *Going Dark* (Fuel Theatre); *Orpheus* (NYT); *Tiger Country* (Hampstead Theatre); *The King and I* (Leicester Curve); *Desire Under the Elms* (New Vic Staffordshire); *Seize the Day* (Tricycle); *Tales of Ballycumber* (Abbey Theatre Dublin); *It's a Wonderful Life* (Wolsey Theatre Ipswich); *The Mountaintop* (Trafalgar Studios); *Just Add Water* (SJDC); *The Ring Cycle* (ROH); *Sugar Mummies, Hitchcock Blonde* (Royal Court); *Julius Caesar* (Barbican); *Richard II* (Old Vic); *The Woman in White* (Palace Theatre, Marquis Theatre NY); *His Dark Materials, Henry V, Jumpers, The Powerbook* (National).

John Tucker – Voice Coach
John runs a London voice studio (www.john-tucker.com), is Voice Associate at HighTide Festival Theatre and a member of the teaching faculty at BADA and teaches at RADA. John has also taught at CSSD and Drama Centre. Previous credits for the Gate include: *Electra, How To Be An Other Woman.* Other theatre credits include: *A Midsummer Night's Dream* (Headlong); *Aristo* (Chichester Festival Theatre); *Certain*

Dark Things (Arcola); *Lidless* (Trafalgar Studios); *Ditch* (Old Vic); *Mother Courage* (ETT); *Shallow Slumber* (Soho Theatre); *Stovepipe* (National Theatre); *The Stronger* (Edinburgh). TV includes: *Classical Star* (BBC).

The Gate would like to thank the following Egyptians who agreed to be interviewed as part of the research for this play: Khalid Abdalla, Mohammed Abdelhammed, Mohammed Abdul Razeq, Dalia Adel, Iman Ahmed, Khaled Al-Barri, Mohammed Salah Ali, Yasmin Ebada, Emad El-Bahat, Sanya El-Bahat, Mansoura Ez-Eldin, Mohammed Hashim, Mustafa Hussein, Christine Jamal, Nadia Montasser, Salma Said, Sondos Shabayak, Laila Soliman.

The Gate would also like to thank the following people for their help with the development of this production: Cathy Costain, Kate Denby, Nouri Hussain, Stuart Hendry at the Glengoyne Distiller, Mark Goddard, Great Queen Street Restaurant, London Bubble, Iona Firouzabadi for MisFit Films, the Mosireen Collective, National Theatre, Notting Hill Blag Club, Rob and all at Object Construction, Paines Plough, the staff at the Prince Albert Pub, Theatre503, Cressida Trew, the Gate Theatre's volunteer ushers and all those who gave their help after this programme had gone to print.

GATE
THEATRE NOTTING HILL

"Queue, cajole or fight to get into this theatre"
The Sunday Times

The Gate is the UK's only small-scale theatre dedicated to producing a repertoire with a wholly international focus, meaning it occupies a unique position within Britain's diverse theatrical landscape. With an average audience capacity of 70, the Gate continues to challenge and inspire artists, making it famous for being one of London's most flexible and transformable theatre spaces.

For over 30 years, the Gate has been a powerhouse in British theatre, serving as a unique engine-room for talent. From directors at the early stages of their careers to exceptional actors, writers and designers all eager to create innovative and inspiring work, the Gate has always been a home for the spirited and anarchic souls of British theatre.

As the Gate's newest Artistic Director, Christopher Haydon continues the Gate's tradition of creating first-class and original theatre.

The Gate Theatre Company is a company limited by guarantee.
Registered in England & Wales No. 1495543 | Charity No. 280278
Registered address: 11 Pembridge Road, Above the Prince Albert Pub, London, W11 3HQ

Support the Gate

A 70 seat theatre tucked away above the Prince Albert pub, the Gate has always punched above its weight. Within one of the most flexible and transformable spaces in London we create bold international theatre and are dedicated to nurturing new theatrical talent. A theatre of our size relies upon the loyalty of our supporters who love our work, spread the word about our shows and give generously to help fulfil our artistic ambitions. We would love you to join us.

For more information on our Supporters' Scheme, please contact Priya Jethwa on 020 7229 5387 or email gate@gatetheatre.co.uk.

The Gate would like to thank the following for their continued generous support:

GATE GUARDIANS Katrina & Chris Barter, Miles Morland, Jon & NoraLee Sedmak, Anda & Bill Winters.

GATE KEEPERS Lauren Clancy, Charles Cormick & Steven Wheeler, Robert Devereux & Vanessa Branson, Cory Edelman, Leslie Feeney, Nick Ferguson, Joachim Fleury, Faith Savage & Michael Gollner, Marianne Hinton, Linda & David Lakhdhir, Tony Mackintosh, Kate Maltby, David Pike, Pascale Revert & Peter Wheeler, David & Susie Sainsbury, The Ulrich Family and 2 Anonymous donors.

GATE LOVERS Anonymous, Rupert Christiansen, Catherine & Edward Faulks, Susan Gibson & Mark Bergman, Jan & Rick Grandison, Kate Grimond, Stephen & Jennifer Harper, Mr & Mrs Michael Kelly, Bill & Stephanie Knight, James & Anne-Marie Mackay, Midge & Simon Palley, Herschel & Peggy Post, Leopold de Rothschild, Gregg Sando & Sarah Havens, Paddy & Jacky Sellers.

Special thanks to Jenny Hall.

TRUSTS & FOUNDATIONS Arts Council England, Jerwood Charitable Foundation, OAK Foundation, Royal Borough of Kensington & Chelsea.

Jerwood Young Designers

The Prophet **Designer: Holly Pigott**

Since 2001 Jerwood Young Designers has given outstanding young designers the opportunity to work on productions in the versatile space of the Gate Theatre in Notting Hill.

The Gate has long had a reputation as having one of the most versatile studio spaces in London, perfect for young designers to explore theatrical possibilities. They also have the chance to work with some of the finest directors and writers working in theatre, an experience which is invaluable in establishing reputation and contacts.

The support that the Jerwood Young Designers scheme provides in both nurturing talent and offering the opportunity of practical experience has been instrumental in launching the careers of some of the country's most exciting theatrical designers.

www.jerwoodcharitablefoundation.org

Hassan Abdulrazzak

THE PROPHET

OBERON BOOKS
LONDON

WWW.OBERONBOOKS.COM

First published in 2012 by Oberon Books Ltd
521 Caledonian Road, London N7 9RH
Tel: +44 (0) 20 7607 3637 / Fax: +44 (0) 20 7607 3629
e-mail: info@oberonbooks.com
www.oberonbooks.com

A catalogue record for this book is available from the British Library.

PB ISBN: 978-1-84943-449-2
Digital ISBN: 978-1-84943-538-3

Cover image © George Henton www.negativespace.asia

Printed, bound and converted
by CPI Group (UK) Ltd, Croydon, CR0 4YY.

Characters

LAYLA

HISHAM

HANI

SUZANNE

METWALI

Act One

SCENE 1

Friday 28th January 2011, 8 a.m. A middle-class apartment in Cairo. HISHAM and LAYLA are a couple in their 30s.

LAYLA: I wish I could say that the first thing I thought about this morning was the revolution. But instead I woke up asking myself one simple question: should I shave off my pubic hair? You see some women here, some brides, they shave it all off, for their husbands on their wedding night. I never did it for Hisham. I always thought that stuff was beneath me. Maybe I should have done it. Maybe it's not too late. We haven't had sex in three months. Is that too long? The gaps between our love making keep getting longer and longer. Sometimes I fear that my vagina will one day just completely clam up, never to open again. I should shave my pubes, I really should. 'Pubic hair' it's a funny phrase, funny word 'pubic', sounds so much like public, doesn't it? Public hair. I mean don't get me wrong generally I'm against privatisation…but public hair, your pubes open to the public, to be seen by the public whenever they please, even for a lefty like me that's going too far. There's no getting around it. We are stagnant. Hisham and me. Sexually and spiritually stagnant. Which is why I was suspicious this morning about his rendezvous.

HISHAM: She didn't.

LAYLA: She did. She crossed the hall.

HISHAM: She was just…

LAYLA: What?

HISHAM: Strolling.

LAYLA: Strolling? At the British Council.

HISHAM: I don't know. Pick another word…the point is –

LAYLA: The point is she crossed the hall to get to you. And she totally ignored me.

HISHAM: Not totally. Look –

LAYLA: No you look. I don't like you seeing her. And why in a hotel?

HISHAM: This is Cairo. Everybody meets in hotels.

LAYLA: Since when? We don't meet our friends in hotels.

HISHAM: Because they're our friends.

LAYLA: I don't like it Hisham.

HISHAM: It's very sweet, all this, and very unlike you…

LAYLA: What do you mean?

HISHAM: Jealousy. After seven years of marriage, one kind of misses it.

LAYLA: I'm not jealous Hisham. This is different. She's a foreigner.

HISHAM: What difference does that –

LAYLA: She's a Westerner.

HISHAM: Now you're just being racist.

LAYLA: She crossed the hall…like this…

LAYLA imitates SUZANNE's walk.

HISHAM: What's with the pouting?

LAYLA: She pouted.

HISHAM: She didn't.

LAYLA: I saw her with my own eyes.

HISHAM: Your imagination is something –

LAYLA: *(Imitating SUZANNE.)* Are you Mr. Hisham Mourad? I loved your novel!

HISHAM sighs.

And you. I swear I could hear it plop.

HISHAM: What?

LAYLA: Your third ball, I could hear it plopping. Whenever someone praises you, it just plops, your third ball. It pushes the other two balls out of the way and folds its little ball arms in total smugness. I heard it.

HISHAM: I was flattered. So what?

LAYLA: Why do you want to see her? Just answer me that.

HISHAM: Come on. Look; it's simple. When the AUP publish the English translation of my first novel I'm going to get a lot more exposure. God knows I need it. I mean sometimes I think only a select few critics even know of its existence.

LAYLA: Rubbish. You did well. As well as any first-time writer can hope for.

HISHAM: Oh yes. Our wonderful publishing industry really took care of me. They don't even tell me how many copies have been sold… Getting translated is everything.

LAYLA: Ah, you've always had this complex.

HISHAM: What complex?

LAYLA: Everything Western is so wonderful. Everything Egyptian is shit.

HISHAM: Is there anyone that doesn't think that?

LAYLA: I don't believe you.

HISHAM: You could be a bestselling author in Egypt and you still can't quit your day job because the publishing house cheats you out of your royalties. Look at Naguib Mahfouz, a Nobel Prize yet he remained a civil servant most of his life. Or Alaa Al-Aswany, he still works as a dentist.

LAYLA: That's because he likes being a dentist –

HISHAM: O rubbish.

LAYLA: Every interview I've seen with him, he always goes on about how his patients provide inspiration.

HISHAM: Gingivitis is never inspiring. I'm telling you, getting translated to English is everything – it's going to open so many doors.

LAYLA: What's you getting translated got to do with her?

HISHAM: There will be a demand for my second novel. I need to finish it.

LAYLA: Yes. Fine. But what do you need her for?

HISHAM: You heard her, she said she could help me with it.

LAYLA: There's nothing wrong with your new novel –

HISHAM: Layla. You haven't even read it.

LAYLA: I skimmed. It's great.

HISHAM: I'm blocked.

LAYLA: You keep saying that.

HISHAM: I keep saying it because I'm blocked.

LAYLA: It makes you sound like a toilet, you do know that.

HISHAM: Thanks. Look I need to get that second novel out. We're running out of money.

LAYLA: I have my job. And you could always go back to Al-Ahram.

HISHAM: Are you kidding, the minute I handed in my resignation there was a feeding frenzy about who would replace me. Besides, I don't want to go back. I have to make this writing thing work. There's no alternative.

LAYLA: I'm fed up Hisham. I don't see why your writing has to come before everything else. I don't see why I just have to accept that.

HISHAM: Hey, hey, what's going on? Why are you so upset?

LAYLA: Something about her makes me uncomfortable.

HISHAM: Suzanne?

LAYLA: Who else.

HISHAM: And what is it that makes you uncomfortable?

LAYLA: She's a hybrid. I don't trust hybrids.

HISHAM: What are you on about? Hybrid?

LAYLA: Half English, half Egyptian…doesn't even speak proper Arabic and to top it all she has the same name as Mubarak's wife…Suzanne. Yuk.

HISHAM: Oh well. You've convinced me. I'm cancelling the appointment right away.

LAYLA: Fine. Fine. Go. You'll sulk forever if you don't and accuse me of getting in the way of your writing career which is what you always do anyway –

HISHAM: I don't accuse you of that.

LAYLA: Just go. But here is what I don't understand Hisham. You've been writing about a revolution, a theoretical revolution this past year.

HISHAM: Year and a half.

LAYLA: And now there is an actual revolution –

HISHAM: No there isn't.

LAYLA: We should have been there on the 25th. Instead we stayed in our flat while thousands took to the streets.

HISHAM: And the police drove them out of Tahrir Square after midnight. The same will happen today.

LAYLA: With that kind of optimism, how could we possibly fail.

HISHAM: They've shut down the internet.

LAYLA: What? When?

HISHAM: It happened last night. I was in the middle of researching something about torture, you know for the scene with Metwali in the book, when suddenly it all went kaput. Is there anything more annoying than those five words 'The page cannot be found'.

LAYLA is trying Twitter on her phone.

LAYLA: Twitter is down.

HISHAM: It looks like they're going for a total communication blackout.

LAYLA: The phones are still working.

HISHAM: Why are you leaving so early? The demos won't start till after the Friday prayer.

LAYLA: I'm going to work first. Hani called me. Sounded worried.

HISHAM: I read on the internet they're calling it the day of rage. It makes it sound like a Kung Fu movie.

(In a film advert voice.) DAY OF RAGE!

LAYLA: You should come with me…Wael will be there.

Beat.

HISHAM: Wael?

LAYLA: You sound surprised.

HISHAM: It's been a while since I heard you say his name. Is that why you are going?

LAYLA: No. Not only because of him. If we, who have opposed the regime for so long don't go down to the streets then who will.

HISHAM: Do you still have feelings for him?

LAYLA: How could you ask me that?

HISHAM: It's alright. You can tell me.

LAYLA: Wael was a part of my life, an important part of my life but that was a long time ago.

HISHAM: I wonder if he has changed.

LAYLA: Come with me and find out.

HISHAM: I don't think so.

LAYLA: I'll call you later. Maybe you can join me after you're done with Suzanne.

HISHAM: Layla, promise me you'll be careful.

LAYLA: I promise.

HISHAM kisses her on the forehead. She leans closer as if wanting him to kiss her on the lips but HISHAM moves away.

SCENE 2

LAYLA: I caught the taxi van at the end of our road. It's a lot cheaper than a cab and more comfortable than a bus. At least in a taxi van, you're not pressed against someone's armpit or worse have some sexually repressed pervert rub himself against you. Of course the answer could be to wear a hijab but I refuse to do that on principle. I've always thought God, if he exists, surely must have bigger fish to fry than worrying about how women should wear their hair. That's the concern of a coiffure, not the creator of everything.

Pause.

On a weekday at this hour, the traffic in Cairo would usually be packed. Bumper to bumper, horns blaring constantly, pedestrians crossing at any point along the road and darting between the cars like a herd of suicidal sheep. But today is Friday. The weekend. And it started like any other Friday, relatively quiet. But there was a palpable sense of anticipation, you could see it on the faces of passers-by. I would rather not have gone into work but I had no choice after Hani's call. In Egypt, you're always aware that standing right behind you is a long line of the unemployed, all looking over your shoulder, craving your job. And the management knows that only too well.

HANI: Layla.

LAYLA: That's my boss, Hani.

HANI: Can I see you in my office for a second.

LAYLA: Sure.

They are in HANI's office.

HANI: How are you?

LAYLA: I'm well. Why did you ask me to come in?

HANI: I'll explain.

LAYLA: Hani, I don't like you calling me at home.

HANI: I'm sorry…I had no choice. Are you going?

Goes to check no one is listening at the door.

HANI: You've heard about the marches, right?

LAYLA: Yes, of course.

HANI: Till a few days ago, I didn't even know Khaled Said had a page on Facebook.

LAYLA: 'We are all Khaled Said'.

HANI: You knew about it?

LAYLA: It's been in the papers.

HANI: Not the ones I read.

LAYLA: I mean in the opposition papers. It's not the only Facebook group, there are others. They're all calling for marches to Tahrir Square.

HANI: I take it you're going?

LAYLA: Oh God, is there…

HANI: What?

LAYLA: Some company policy about not going to political rallies.

HANI: No, no, of course not. Vodafone is a forward-looking company.

LAYLA: Oh good.

HANI: It would be totally draconian…

LAYLA: Yes.

HANI: This is a Western company, things like freedom, democracy and equality, they come with our company like Nokia accessories.

LAYLA: That's great.

HANI: Did you see the two men who were just here?

LAYLA: Laurel and Hardy.

HANI: Yes.

LAYLA: What about them?

HANI: State security.

LAYLA: Really?

HANI: The fat one kept smoking the whole time, dropped ash everywhere.

HANI picks up some of the ash and puts it in a small plant he has on his desk.

LAYLA: What are you doing?

HANI: I don't have an ashtray.

LAYLA: You'll kill the cactus.

HANI: I think it's already dead. It's hard to tell with cacti. They just sit there in the pot like a disgruntled relative.

LAYLA: What did you want to talk to me about?

HANI: Why are you in such a hurry?

LAYLA shrugs, she wants to go on the march.

I thought you might have changed your mind. It's not a good idea you know.

LAYLA: If everyone thought that then nothing will ever change.

25

HANI: I'm just worried about you. I don't want you to be harmed.

LAYLA: Is this what you wanted to talk to me about?

HANI: No, there's something else.

HANI goes to the door, checks no one is listening.

Sit down.

LAYLA: I'm fine standing up.

HANI: Stop being like that Layla.

LAYLA: Like what?

HANI: Everything I say, you go against it. What harm would come from sitting down for God's sake?

LAYLA: Fine, fine. I'll sit.

LAYLA takes a seat.

HANI: Would you like some lemonade. I could get Abdulrahman to bring you –

LAYLA: I'm fine really – Hani just tell me what did the state security want –

HANI: He makes excellent lemonade –

LAYLA: Hani!

HANI: Right. Well they were very polite. I didn't expect that. I haven't had much dealing with state security before. To tell the truth I've never had dealings with them. I'm not political, I've got nothing against Mubarak. Thank God I had his portrait up, that was a stroke of luck. I was thinking of removing it –

LAYLA: I can't stand to look at him.

HANI: He doesn't bother me, it's just the eyes follow you everywhere, you know. It makes you feel guilty even when you have nothing to feel guilty about. I was lucky that I didn't remove it, I came close last week, anyway God averted that disaster because the state security men did look at the portrait, oh yes and they gave me a kind of approving nod.

LAYLA: Wonderful to know you all basked in the glory of Mubarak. Can I go now?

HANI: Wait, I haven't finished. Fine I'll tell you. They asked us to shut down the network.

LAYLA: What?

HANI: The mobile phone network.

LAYLA: They can't.

HANI: They're state security, they can do whatever the hell they like.

LAYLA: It's bad enough they have switched off the internet. How are the demonstrators supposed to keep in touch with each other?

HANI: They're not. That the point. I think they intend to crush the revolt.

LAYLA: Well I hope you told them to go to hell.

HANI: What?

LAYLA: We're not shutting down the network.

HANI: Layla, we're not in some kind of American movie –

LAYLA: My God, you capitulated.

HANI: You're not Julia Roberts playing Erin Brockovich. You're in Egypt, my love, where saying no to state security means getting your balls electrocuted. I like mine just the way they are, medium rare. Now as my senior engineer, you would be best qualified to –

LAYLA: Absolutely not –

HANI: Layla, if the government wants us to shut down the phones, there's nothing we can do –

LAYLA: There is. We can resist.

HANI: They'll only pull the plug themselves and you know that it will be much more difficult to turn the network back on once they do that.

LAYLA: Ask someone else Hani –

HANI: I'm asking you. You do want to keep this job, don't you?

LAYLA: Are you threatening me?

HANI: You should be grateful you have a job like this.

LAYLA: What happened to democracy and freedom coming like phone accessories with this company –

HANI: What?

LAYLA: That's what you just told me.

HANI: Did I?

LAYLA: Are they asking all phone companies to do the same?

HANI: I don't know. I didn't ask. But it makes sense to approach us first, we're the biggest. And besides we've got that funky red logo.

LAYLA: Say no.

HANI: I can't.

LAYLA: Have some spine, Hani and say no.

HANI: I called London.

LAYLA: And?

HANI: They said we can't afford to upset the Egyptian government, that I'm to do whatever is asked of me.

LAYLA: Cowards!

HANI: I think the word you're looking for is 'pragmatists'.

LAYLA: Ahh, this is exactly what I hate about the West. They go on and on about freedom and democracy but when push comes to shove –

HANI: Hold your horses there Naomi Klein. That kind of talk is not going to help anyone. We need to pull the plug and we need to do it now.

LAYLA: No.

HANI: I can't ask anyone else.

LAYLA: Why not?

HANI: I don't trust them with doing it right. We've never shut down our entire network before.

LAYLA: Hani, find someone –

HANI: OK, calm down and listen to me for a minute. Wouldn't you rather the job is done right so that if we are asked to switch on the network, we can do so quickly...think about it. *(Whispering.)* This is a bit of a dumb move on the part of the government.

The cactus catches his attention again, he pushes it away.

LAYLA: What are you doing?

HANI: I think the cactus is bugged.

LAYLA: Oh come off it.

HANI: The thin one kept playing with it the whole time. Maybe he was planting a mic.

LAYLA: Maybe they bugged your office weeks or months earlier, maybe years, maybe they've been listening to you since you got this job.

HANI: O my God, do you think?

LAYLA: Ah Hani, just say no. *(Picks up the cactus and speaks into it.)* No, fuck you.

HANI: Stop!

LAYLA: What, you expect some helicopters to land on the roof and a SWAT team to break in through the window? I have news for you, you're not Keanu Reeves.

LAYLA is about to leave the office.

HANI: Wait…wait…OK, fine. I'll say it loud, I don't care who is listening.

(Into the cactus.) The government is stupid.

(Puts the cactus down.) Shutting us down is going to guarantee that we are the headline story around the world for the next twenty-four hours. So actually you Layla…by executing this little bit of oppression will end up helping the demonstrators in their cause. What, you don't believe me? Just think about it.

SCENE 3

HISHAM is sitting at his writing desk, looking out of the window. He gets up, tucks his chair back into the desk, picks up his jacket from the back of the chair and puts it on.

Now he is in a hotel. Sounds of elevator, hum of guests, etc could he heard.

HISHAM sits on a sofa chair.

Enter SUZANNE (wearing a red coat).

SUZANNE: Hisham!

HISHAM gets up to his feet. They shake hands.

SUZANNE: Sorry I'm late. My driver turned up a whole hour later than he was supposed to. I'm staying in one of those horrid gated compounds on the outskirts of the city so it always takes me – Have you had something to drink?

HISHAM: No.

SUZANNE: Great. I'll order something. I'm feeling a bit parched myself. How have you been?

HISHAM: Well…

SUZANNE: I read your manuscript.

HISHAM: Great. And what did you make of it?

SUZANNE: We'll get to that. First let's order some drinks. What would you like?

HISHAM: I don't know…coffee perhaps.

SUZANNE: Hmm… No, let's be really decadent and order something a little stronger, what do you say?

HISHAM: I don't really drink this early.

SUZANNE: Neither do I but there's something about hotels isn't there that just makes you want to order something alcoholic.

HISHAM: Yes I think I know what you mean. I wonder why that is.

SUZANNE: Advertising. I was in advertising before I switched. It's amazing how that stuff just infiltrates. Someone comes up with a whiskey ad in Madison Avenue and here we are in Cairo, thousands of miles away, falling under its influence. Soft lighting, plush chairs and immediately we think of single malt.

HISHAM: So that's how you started, I mean before you became a literary agent, you were in advertising?

SUZANNE: Yes. It's the same thing really. Except now I have just one type of product I'm trying to promote. Authors and their books.

HISHAM: Not sure I like being thought of in that way.

SUZANNE: What way?

HISHAM: As a product.

SUZANNE: OK, you're not a washing-up liquid or a tooth brush, I give you that. Actually I always see writers as being closer to single malt. A kind of dignified product that leaves a rich taste in one's throat. I'm making you uncomfortable. Let's order.

SUZANNE looks at the drinks menu. HISHAM picks up his copy.

I've decided. You?

HISHAM: I think I'll go for that single malt.

SUZANNE: Aha, the power of suggestion. It never fails.

SUZANNE snaps her fingers, a waiter stops.

A Bellini, extra chilled and a single, make that double Glengoyne...on the rocks?

HISHAM: Neat.

SUZANNE: Neat. Thanks.

Waiter nods and goes to fetch the drinks. HISHAM looks at the waiter.

What's wrong?

HISHAM: Nothing, he reminded me of someone. My wife's boss.

SUZANNE: He's kind of handsome. In a boyish, Keanu Reeves sort of way.

HISHAM: Yes, that's the trouble.

SUZANNE: What do you mean?

HISHAM: Nothing.

SUZANNE: You think your wife is having an affair with her boss?

HISHAM: *(With decreasing assertiveness.)* No...no...no.

SUZANNE: Oh dear. Do you think they come to a hotel like this?

HISHAM: My wife is not having an affair.

Brief silence.

SUZANNE: Hotels...marvellous places. I love to roam a hotel really late at night. Have you ever done that? Once I stayed in a hotel in Dubai and realized it was linked to some five other hotels by all these glass tunnels. It was like being in a city within a city. So I'd walk around going from one lobby to the next. A Jazz pianist would be playing here, a group of business men watching a baseball game there. Just wonderful to roam all that space. And then later at night everything would get real quiet. Just a handful of night owl guests staying up. Maybe an adulterous couple sitting in the corner sipping their drinks, flirting. Then later still there would be no one around. Just me and the sound of my shoes going from lobby to lobby to lobby. But do you know what the best part of staying in a hotel is?

HISHAM: What?

SUZANNE: The power you have over other people, to know you can order them to fetch you something, anything, even late into the night. It is a thrill.

HISHAM: Is it?

SUZANNE: Don't tell me you've never had power over someone else. Having read your novel I thought you might have.

HISHAM: Really why is that?

SUZANNE: Your dictator character, he was very plausible.

HISHAM: Well…I suppose I was drawing on a certain president…

SUZANNE: Of course.

They both look at the portrait of Mubarak hanging on the wall.

They do it more subtly in other dictatorships. You've been to Cuba, haven't you?

HISHAM: Over ten years ago, how could you possibly know –

SUZANNE: You must have noticed that Fidel unlike Mubarak doesn't have his portrait everywhere. The figure you see the most is Che Guevara and who could possibly be mad at the handsome, permanently youthful and permanently dead Guevara? Mubarak, on the other hand, behaves like the Pharaohs. All public traces of his predecessors must be erased. There is only him, oh and of course his son. Yes I thought you got under the skin of the dictator really well.

HISHAM: I wasn't drawing on Mubarak alone. There were some ex-bosses, little Mubaraks you could call them, which also provided inspiration.

SUZANNE: You started working for Al-Ahram, didn't you, straight after you graduated?

HISHAM: Yes how –

SUZANNE: I make a point of studying all my potential clients.

HISHAM: Are you thinking of taking me on?

SUZANNE: That very much depends on you Hisham. Working with me won't be easy. I tend to batter the egos of my clients. And with you it will be a rough ride. Are you sure you want to go through with it?

HISHAM: You mean you have harsh notes for me?

Pause.

SUZANNE: Tell me in a sentence what your novel is about?

HISHAM: It's a family saga…

SUZANNE: No, no, no. Don't describe the components. Just get to the heart of it. What's it about?

HISHAM: I suppose –

SUZANNE: Don't suppose. The heart of it, Hisham. Think of it as a movie and you have to come up with a tag line. What would it be?

HISHAM: You can't reduce –

SUZANNE: Nonsense. Everything can be reduced to one line. That's the first rule of advertising. What's the heart of your novel, come on.

HISHAM: Revolution in Egypt.

SUZANNE: Good. Lousy tag line of course but at least we're getting somewhere. And how do you envisage this revolution would take place.

HISHAM: The story is allegorical…

SUZANNE: Goes without saying –

HISHAM: And in early drafts I thought perhaps a figure would rise from amongst the opposition parties.

SUZANNE: Then you realized…

HISHAM: It's never going to happen.

SUZANNE: And why is that?

HISHAM: With the exception of the Muslim Brotherhood, the other parties, the secular parties, they don't really have a connection with the people.

SUZANNE: Exactly.

HISHAM: So for a powerful leader to rise from amongst them at this stage, it's too far-fetched.

SUZANNE: Counterfactual.

HISHAM: Yes.

SUZANNE: And with fiction, you have to have one foot in reality.

HISHAM: Yes or even both feet.

SUZANNE: No. One foot in reality and one foot on a ladder up to the stars. If you want both feet in reality then go and make a documentary, you have no business being in the business of fiction. I think you know that, hence your flight of fancy.

HISHAM: Sorry what do you mean?

SUZANNE: The mysterious saviour figure who appears halfway through the book.

HISHAM: Yes.

SUZANNE: A kind of religious cocktail, one part Jesus, two parts Muhammad, shaken, stirred and garnished with a touch of Buddha.

HISHAM laughs.

Do you really think this is how the revolution will start?

HISHAM: I don't know. I don't even know if we will ever have a revolution.

SUZANNE: They say there'll be record numbers on the street today. This could be the start.

HISHAM: I doubt it.

SUZANNE: Why so cynical?

HISHAM: I'm not cynical, just a realist. I've been involved with opposition politics most of my life.

SUZANNE: But you were never jailed, is that right?

HISHAM: Er…yes, that's true.

SUZANNE: Go on.

HISHAM: What was I saying?

SUZANNE: How you were involved in opposition politics most of your life.

HISHAM: Yes and many times, I felt we were on the brink of something. When the Kefaya movement started trying to put a stop to Mubarak passing on the presidency to his son Gamal. I really thought things might change, that Mubarak might finally leave the throne…but even they ran out of steam. And he's still here, Mubarak, like a heavy blanket over all of us.

SUZANNE: You've never been an activist.

HISHAM: I'm a writer…I see my task as primarily listening, jotting things down. And even in my political articles, I'm more of a describer of the problems I see. I leave the solutions to others.

SUZANNE: So you'll stick your neck out so far but no further.

HISHAM: Ouch.

SUZANNE: Sorry. That was too harsh. Actually I have read some of your articles and you are quite critical of the regime. Don't you worry they might arrest you?

HISHAM: Ever since the US put pressure on Mubarak to be more pluralistic, the regime has allowed us writers some degree of freedom. We have the freedom to talk and they have the freedom not to listen. So, no, I'm not worried.

Waiter sets down their drinks. SUZANNE takes a big gulp. HISHAM sips his whiskey.

SUZANNE: But they could arrest you at any time.

HISHAM: I suppose they could.

SUZANNE: Just kidnap you, maybe even in broad daylight. They've done it to others.

HISHAM: Nothing in life is ever risk free.

SUZANNE: You are a brave man.

HISHAM: There are many others who are much braver and condemn the regime in much harsher tones than me.

SUZANNE: And modest also. I think I'm going to enjoy working with you. How about we start right away?

HISHAM: Yes I'd love to hear your thoughts about the novel.

SUZANNE: No, let's set the novel aside for a moment. What I'm prepared to offer –

HISHAM takes out his phone.

HISHAM: Sorry.

SUZANNE: What?

HISHAM: I thought I felt my phone vibrating.

SUZANNE: You're expecting a call?

HISHAM: Yes from my wife. False alarm.

SUZANNE: Oh yes, I met her at the British Council dinner. What's her name?

HISHAM: Layla.

SUZANNE: I always have a problem remembering the names of my client's wives. She won't get through to you. They've shut down the network.

HISHAM: What? Since when?

SUZANNE: An hour ago. Haven't you noticed?

HISHAM: No.

SUZANNE: The landlines are working but the internet and mobiles are down.

HISHAM: That's a bad sign.

SUZANNE: A lot of bones will be broken before the day is out. I hope your wife is not out on the street.

HISHAM: I'm afraid she is.

SUZANNE: How come you didn't join her?

HISHAM: I wanted to keep our appointment.

SUZANNE: Well I'm deeply flattered…I remember your wife, pretty girl. But looked bored at that dinner.

HISHAM: She's an engineer. She finds the literary world…

SUZANNE: Pretentious.

HISHAM: Fake, I think that's the word she uses.

SUZANNE: And so it is. Which is why good advice is so hard to come by.

HISHAM: And I suppose that is what you are offering me?

SUZANNE: Our London branch is looking for talent from the Middle East. This is a departure. Usually when we seek foreign writers we skip over the Arabs and look for them in South America, Japan or Eastern Europe. But things are changing. There is a recognition that it is not good to continue ignoring this area. That the things we ignore have a habit of popping up later, when we least expect them to, armed with sharp teeth ready to bite us. How is your drink?

HISHAM: Sorry.

SUZANNE: The whiskey.

HISHAM: It's making me light-headed.

SUZANNE: Good.

HISHAM: Why is that good?

SUZANNE: It will make you more receptive to the process.

HISHAM: What process?

SUZANNE: Your new novel, the manuscript you sent me, it's unfinished…

HISHAM: Yes.

SUZANNE: You are blocked.

HISHAM nods.

Like I told you at the dinner, I could help with that. Unblock you so to speak. But you have to be open to my process. Are you free this afternoon?

HISHAM: I was hoping –

SUZANNE: It's just that my time is limited and I'm keen for us to start as soon as possible. I might have to go back to London at any moment. Anyway we won't take that long.

HISHAM: In that case, yes I guess I'm free.

SUZANNE: Wonderful. I'm sure I can make it worth your while.

SCENE 4

HANI's office. LAYLA is about to leave.

HANI: Layla…can I see you for a second.

Reluctantly LAYLA enters the office. Pause.

HANI: Thank you.

LAYLA: I feel terrible.

HANI: Don't.

LAYLA: I can't believe you made me do that.

HANI: It's done now.

LAYLA: You always make do things that I regret later.

HANI: I keep thinking back to Dalia's Christmas party.

LAYLA: Hani, please don't start –

HANI: Wait, hear me out.

LAYLA: No, I made a mistake. I told you that. We both had too much to drink.

HANI: I know…I know…

LAYLA: I love Hisham.

HANI: I know…all I'm asking is…

LAYLA: What?

HANI: Come with me to Sharm el-Sheikh for the weekend.

LAYLA: You're out of your mind.

HANI: Wait, it's not –

LAYLA: I'm a married woman…

HANI: Hisham doesn't love you.

LAYLA: How dare you –

HANI: What husband leaves his wife to go to a Christmas party by herself?

LAYLA: He was busy, working –

HANI: If you were mine, I would never leave you –

LAYLA: Hani.

HANI: Hear me out for a second. I just want your company, that's all. In Sharm, we'll have separate rooms, it will all be above board. I just want to spend a weekend with you, swimming, talking, having dinner together.

LAYLA: Forget it.

LAYLA is about to leave the office.

HANI: OK bring Hisham with you.

LAYLA: What? Is this some sick fantasy of yours?

HANI: No.

LAYLA: The world's most awkward threesome.

HANI: No, no, no, listen –

LAYLA: Hani, I made a mistake once. I was vulnerable. I think you and I just need –

HANI: Will you listen…I'll bring a date. Mimi, or someone, I don't know. And we'll go, all four of us. It doesn't matter to me. I just want to be around you. I'd rather you made an excuse, tell Hisham you're visiting your sister in Alexandria and you and I go off on our own to Sharm. But if that is asking too much then fine. Let's play it like a double date. I'll pay for everything.

LAYLA: How do you want me to justify that to Hisham?

HANI: I'll invite you both over to dinner. And in the course of the evening, I'll tell him I have this discount for the Hilton at Sharm, I mean we'll just figure something out. The main thing is that we will be together.

LAYLA: Nothing can come of this.

HANI: I know that. Like I said, I just want to be around you. What I'm asking for is totally platonic. It's really just to get around the annoying social barrier to what ought to be something perfectly natural.

LAYLA: What are you talking about?

HANI: For a married woman to have some male friends. You know that I spent some time in London, right. And there it's normal. Everywhere you go, married men and women meeting friends of the opposite sex.

LAYLA: Really?

HANI: Absolutely. They go on holiday together, totally fine with their spouses. It's even understood that if they accidentally ended up making love – don't look at me like that, I'm describing what happens in London. It's understood that acting on the sexual impulse is acceptable. That's how they see it in the West. They don't have our repressions. Now that's what I call real freedom.

LAYLA: You're a man, of course you would.

HANI: It will take us a hundred years to catch up. But you and I, we can hurry things a little bit, can't we? I mean you do like me, otherwise what happened between us could never have happened. Am I right?

LAYLA nods.

There is a certain amount of chemistry. Perfectly natural, doesn't mean you don't love Hisham or anything. It just means, you are the sort of woman who likes a tiny bit of spice in her life. Friendships with men. It ought to be a universal right. So what do you say?

LAYLA remains silent.

Don't you want to get away from Cairo, all the traffic, all the noise? Sharm el-Sheikh is like another country. It's the Egypt of our dreams: clean, efficient and best of all the poor pushed right out like someone vacuumed them all up. That's why president Mubarak goes there at every opportunity he gets. It's perfect. You're perfect. So all I want to do is bring two perfect things together.

LAYLA: I have to go.

HANI: I keep remembering that moment of us standing on Dalia's balcony when the clouds parted and suddenly you were bathed in moonlight. So beautiful, so elegant, even though you were wearing that funny little hat.

LAYLA: I was dressed as Sally Bowles from Cabaret.

HANI: I couldn't take my eyes off you.

LAYLA: You caught me on a vulnerable day.

HANI: I think I will carry the taste of your lips to my grave.

LAYLA: Hani…I love Hisham.

HANI: Is he going down to the streets with you?

LAYLA: No. But that's not the point.

HANI: Let me guess, he has work to do. It wouldn't be like this if you were with me.

LAYLA: I have to go.

SCENE 5

HISHAM and SUZANNE arrive at an abandoned building. There are chains attached to the wall. There is a table with the same whiskey bottle they had earlier. They are both laughing.

HISHAM: I shouldn't have had that third glass.

HISHAM puts his hands on his knees.

HISHAM: Phoo.

SUZANNE: Nonsense. Think of Hemingway. There's a whole bar dedicated to him in Havana. That tells you something.

HISHAM: What is this place?…I thought you were taking me to where you are staying.

SUZANNE: I didn't say that.

HISHAM: No I suppose you didn't. This place, it's…

SUZANNE: Familiar.

HISHAM: Yes.

SUZANNE picks up the whiskey bottle.

SUZANNE: Would you care for a top-up?

HISHAM: I don't…

SUZANNE: I'm afraid there are no glasses so…

She tilts her head, opens her mouth then pours some whiskey. It drips down her chin.

Not very dignified. Here, come on. Have some.

HISHAM: I ought to stop.

SUZANNE: Certainly but why start today.

HISHAM takes the bottle, drinks.

Let me guess. You like a drink while you work.

HISHAM: Not always.

SUZANNE: You find it unlocks your subconscious.

HISHAM: Or sends me to sleep. It doesn't always work.

SUZANNE: You have trouble unlocking your subconscious, don't you Hisham. Why is that I wonder?

HISHAM: What makes you say that?

SUZANNE: The manuscript you sent me. It's missing something, isn't it.

HISHAM: That's what I feel.

SUZANNE: It's because you've been holding back.

HISHAM: On what?

SUZANNE: We'll get to that…would you excuse me. I need to make a quick call.

HISHAM wanders around while SUZANNE makes her call. After a while he takes out his phone and looks at it.

(On the phone.) Where are you?….good, no finish your tea, it's fine…we still have some time…I'll text you.

She hangs up.

HISHAM: How did you do that?

SUZANNE: What?

HISHAM: Make a call. The network is still down.

SUZANNE: Magic.

HISHAM: Can I use your phone to call my wife?

SUZANNE: I'm afraid I can't let you do that.

HISHAM: Why not.

SUZANNE: It will violate the spirit of the process. Besides I'm sure your wife is having a blast. A blast with her boss.

HISHAM: What?

SUZANNE: Nothing.

HISHAM: What do you mean 'with her boss'?

SUZANNE: It's just a bit of paranoia I'm sending your way. Is it taking hold?

HISHAM: A little.

SUZANNE: Good. Paranoia must confer a survival advantage, otherwise it wouldn't exist.

HISHAM: *(Regarding the chains on the wall.)* What are these for?

SUZANNE: Christmas decorations.

HISHAM: Seriously.

SUZANNE: I thought you would recognize this place. You got in trouble at Al-Ahram for writing about it.

HISHAM: Wait…no, this isn't the same prison.

SUZANNE: I know it isn't. This place is abandoned. I couldn't exactly take you to a prison cell that was in use, now could I.

HISHAM: But it looks a lot like it. Huh, I thought I was being a real journalist, writing about the torture chambers in our country.

SUZANNE: Our country?

HISHAM: Egypt.

SUZANNE: You forget I'm half British.

HISHAM: You don't consider Egypt your country?

SUZANNE: When I look at a map of the Middle East, I see all the countries shimmering, you know, like someone put them in a pan and turned the heat up. They are unstable, liable to split or merge or get invaded. So yes whilst technically I'm Egyptian, it's just so much easier to say I'm a Brit. Easier to move about in the world and not just because of the passport but because everyone knows that Britain is always going to be there. We have democracy, history and nukes so no one will mess with us.

HISHAM: Egypt has history.

SUZANNE: One out of three.

HISHAM: When I met you at the British Council dinner you were talking very enthusiastically about Egypt.

SUZANNE: Oh with the Brits, I always do that. But there's no point in pretending with other Egyptians.

HISHAM: I do the same.

SUZANNE: I know you do.

HISHAM: How…?

SUZANNE: As I keep saying, I've researched you thoroughly. Now I want you to look again, what does this place remind you of.

HISHAM: I don't know. It's very familiar. It's a bit like the prison cell I wrote about for Al-Ahram but not quite, it's more like…

SUZANNE: The prison cell in your novel.

HISHAM: Yes! That's right.

SUZANNE: Where your prophet character is tortured by that hideous man.

HISHAM: Metwali.

SUZANNE: Yes. He needs more work.

HISHAM: Does he?

SUZANNE: He's too generic. Give him a hobby or something.

HISHAM: He's a torturer.

SUZANNE: Torturers can have hobbies. And your prophet character –

HISHAM: Is he flawed also?

SUZANNE: Who did you base him on?

HISHAM: Why do you want to know?

SUZANNE: Never mind. You'll tell me in time. Are you ready to start Hisham?

HISHAM: I guess.

SUZANNE: My process is really simple. It's about unlocking the subconscious which is every writer's friend and foe. Now I want you to think of yourself as a city. You are a city by the sea in a poor country or maybe in a poor area inside a rich country. You are full of ramshackle housing, substandard schools, awful public transport. You have entire neighbourhoods full of criminals, where the citizens of your city fear to go. This is your mind Hisham. This is what it looks like right now. Cluttered with the poor and the corrupt.

SUZANNE is texting someone while she talks.

Now a hurricane comes or maybe a flood overcomes the city levees or the city gets invaded. It doesn't really matter what the calamity is. When it comes, your citizens run for fear of their lives. They experience a shock to the system, and at this point they are happy to clutch at any straw they could find, anything to end the pain of the calamity. And that's when the repair process begins. Do you follow?

HISHAM: Suzanne…I think I drank too much whiskey –

SUZANNE: It is only when we are at our most vulnerable that the greatest change can be imposed upon us.

Enter METWALI. He strikes HISHAM unconscious.

ACT II

SCENE 1

LAYLA: I was thinking of Hisham when I left the office. Was he with Suzanne now? Was she flirting with him the way Hani had been flirting with me? Were Hisham's defences lowering? My God they're meeting at a hotel! How easy it would be after a couple of drinks to rent a room. How would I know. I can't even call him. Don't judge me, I know, these were not exactly revolutionary thoughts. But this is life, you don't always think about what you're supposed to. I was heading to Tahrir Square and the only thing that was on my mind – for a while at least – was Hisham and our stagnant marriage. That's the truth.

Pause.

I took the metro to Mubarak station hoping to change from line 2 to line 1 so I could reach Naser station near Tahrir Square. But when I got off at Mubarak I was immediately suffocated with tear gas. The police had fired tear gas into the metro station, never mind it was named after our beloved president, that didn't stop them. Everybody was now running out. I went past police with their guard dogs. I couldn't breathe. My eyes were hurting. All exits were shut except one. The police were dictating the direction we were going. When I emerged from the exit, I had no idea where I was. Then it dawned on me that I was in the type of neighbourhood we call ashwaiya, meaning that it is a slum, inhabited by the very poor of Cairo.

Pause.

So picture the scene, a group of suffocated, mainly middle-class Cairenes like myself emerging out of the metro station in the heart of the Egyptian underclass. Marx must have been dancing in his grave with joy. Before me I saw a massive crowd, all determined to head to Tahrir Square but

the streets leading out of the ashwaiya slum were blocked
by police. How to get there? And that's when I saw her,
a girl of sixteen or seventeen, a street girl with a gash on
her cheek, the type that sells Kleenex tissue at traffic lights.
She was guiding us disorientated demonstrators towards
Tahrir. She would run ahead of us, check out the street to
see if it is blocked by the police then run back and lead
us through yet another alleyway. We kept snaking our
way though the slum until we emerged on a main road.
Ahead of us was the Hilton hotel which seemed like a
mad contrast to where we had just been. The crowd was
now getting larger and larger. I noticed many poor women
with us. They were chanting 'long live Egypt' and 'bread,
freedom and social justice'. I never thought women like
these would join the protest. Before the revolution when
I used to go on demos where there were no more than
100 of us, these could have been the very same women
who would spit on us and heap insults. The government
had been very successful at spreading fear against anyone
agitating against the regime. But today was different,
today the barrier of fear came crashing down. It struck
noon and it was time for the Friday prayer. People began
to pray in the street. I thought of joining them, not for
religious reasons, me and God are not on speaking terms
but because it was such a wonderful symbolic moment. We
were claiming the streets for ourselves. Ahead of us were
the police in riot gear and here we were in the middle of
the street, praying. I didn't pray in the end, just stood there
looking at the crowd: men, women and children as far as
the eye could see; even the side streets were flooded with
people. After the prayer ended, we kept on going towards
Tahrir. The police began to fire tear gas at us. I breathed
so much that I nearly collapsed. I retreated a little to get a
breath of fresh air. I saw an empty gas canister and picked
it up. OK, I'll be honest, I was looking for the 'made in the
USA' stamp on it but this one was plain, probably locally
made. Normally I'm all for local produce but obviously not
on this occasion. As we retreated back into the ashwaiya

area, the people there began to open their houses to take
in those who were fainting or tired and give them first aid.
Some of the women stood on their balconies and began
to throw onions down to us. Why? I didn't get it at first,
then I realised the onions were to combat the effect of the
tear gas. Other people in the march were more prepared
than me, they had brought with them cans of Pepsi to wash
their faces with. One guy shared his can with me. When I
asked him how he knew about this he told me that he had
learned it from his Tunisian friends on Facebook. The tear
gas was relentless and just as you combat the effect of one
canister, another would quickly follow. Once again the
poor came to our rescue. They came out of their houses
carrying pots full of vinegar. On the balconies, they were
tearing their bedsheets and throwing it down to us. You
pick up the cloth, soak it in vinegar then put it on your
face for relief. So there I was reeking of onions, Pepsi and
vinegar, thinking this is what freedom smells like. For the
next couple of hours we kept playing cat and mouse with
the police. We would advance a little in the direction of
Tahrir Square and they would push us back with tear gas.
We would retreat, recuperate and then advance again.
Every now and then I would see a demonstrator take out
their phone to check for a signal and a pang of guilt would
sweep through me. What would the demonstrators do to
me if they knew I was the one that pulled the plug on their
phones? Would they attack me? Call me traitor? You have
a certain image of yourself, the things you wouldn't do. But
then life puts that image to the test and you find yourself
wanting.

(Beat.)

The people found a way of keeping the lines of
communication open. They would convey messages to
each other on the street, pass on nuggets of information
they had picked up. One man was shouting: 'Take courage
another march headed from Al-Azhar mosque is on its
way'. Another would warn: 'be careful don't go down
that road, they are arresting protesters there'. It was now

coming up to three, time for the afternoon prayer. People
started chanting 'selmya…selmya', 'peaceful…peaceful',
so that the police would let them pray. Some of the
protesters went over to where the police were standing and
negotiated a truce with one of the lieutenants. The police
ceased firing the tear gas but you could feel they were still
tense and malicious. They had been fighting protesters for
four days in a row and they were getting tired. Nothing had
prepared them for the huge turnout today. Once again the
people before me began to pray and I stood on the sideline
watching them. I kept watching the faces of the police,
trying to read them. As soon as the prayer was over they
began to fire on us. This time not with tear gas but with
live bullets. We ran in a panic where we had come from
but they had put up a metal barrier. People crashed against
it and fell. I fell also and thought I would be crushed to
death. The panic of that moment. The sheer panic. Then
a pair of hands thrust through the crowd and grabbed me.
I was being picked up by a young revolutionary. Later I
learnt his name was Mohammed. He had an afro and wore
his jeans so low his boxer shorts were showing. He carried
me in his arms out of the scrum of collapsed people and to
the safety of the curb. All around us the bullets were flying.
He grabbed my hand and we started running back into
the ashwaiya slum. A door opened and a woman wearing
a red tarha on her head ushered us in. We entered into a
courtyard and saw other demonstrators also taking refuge
there. We found a corner and sat down. We kept listening
to the gunfire and the hiss of the gas canisters. Above us a
helicopter crossed the patch of blue sky that we could see
from the courtyard. The women of the ashwaiya brought
us food. All this time whilst the police was firing on us,
they had been at home cooking for the demonstrators. It
was such a sweet gesture that I was lost for words when
they asked me to tuck in. So there we were a group of
demonstrators from all sort of backgrounds, breaking
bread with these poor women of Cairo. Suddenly the
thought that had popped into my mind this morning, you

know – should I shave my pubic hair? – well it just came back to me. And I thought maybe I could ask those women about it. After all the practice is more common amongst their class than mine. Maybe they'd give me good tips. Use wax, don't use thread, that sort of thing. Or maybe they would offer to remove the hair themselves. Shaving one's pubic hair must surely be a novel way of breaking down class barriers. I can't imagine why no one thought of it before. Or maybe somebody has and I'm just not aware of it. Perhaps it was mentioned in a missing appendix to the communist manifesto. I was almost tempted to ask one of the women about it when suddenly the door of the courtyard flung open and the teenage girl with the gash on her check rushed in, several kids trailing behind her. 'The police are leaving!' she screamed. We all got up and filed out of the courtyard into the streets of the ashwaiya and back towards the Hilton. There was an air of jubilation now as if we had won a decisive battle. One man next to me said 'we beat them'. Then we saw the army arriving with their tanks. My heart sank. I thought this is it. They will start massacring us now. Mohammed was more optimistic. He told me 'don't be scared. This is our army. It's here to protect us'. I thought, he's just a kid, what does he know. I feared the army because the regime paid them to stay loyal. I couldn't see them taking our side. But for now they looked like they were keeping the peace. Mohammed told me he had to leave as his mum and sisters would be worried about him. We hugged. It seemed so natural. Normally I wouldn't hug a man I just met like that on the streets of Cairo but today all the rules and old ways of being had been shredded. We hugged and no one looked at us funny or said an unkind word. I wondered how long things would stay that way. We said our goodbyes and he was gone. I headed towards Tahrir Square.

Pause.

It was getting dark now and a little chilly. Suddenly I noticed that the NDP building was on fire. People were running out of the building carrying monitors and chairs. The scene was like something out of Iraq. Still I can't say I felt sorry to see the headquarters of Mubarak's party on fire. As I approached Tahrir I could see a scrum of people gathered in the centre. Someone had erected a makeshift platform and a man in a wheelchair was being pushed up a ramp on to it.

Optional: In another part of the stage WAEL in his wheelchair and SUZANNE appear. They are facing away from the audience (or obscured in some way).

It was Wael. Wael Said, my ex-boyfriend. And the person pushing him, looked from this distance. It can't be. It was Suzanne or at least a woman that looked like her. A young man handed Wael a megaphone. He tried to speak into it but it wasn't working. He started shouting but I couldn't hear what he was saying. I tried to get closer; there were so many people in front of me it was impossible. Then in another part of the square one young man had climbed up on the shoulders of his friend and began chanting 'down with the regime'. The people around him repeated the chant. Wael was now completely drowned. After a while Suzanne or the woman that looked like Suzanne pushed the chair down the ramp and off the platform. I could no longer see Wael as he was now surrounded by people who seemed to be having a very heated discussion with him. What had he said? I wished I was closer to him. I suddenly remembered the brutal way with which he was treated by the government and it made me want to cry. Then someone tapped me on the shoulder and when I turned I thought for a second it was Hisham.

SCENE 2

HISHAM is tied to the chair. His mouth is stuffed with a cloth and taped. METWALI is finishing his prayer. He gets up, folds his prayer mat neatly, puts it away. HISHAM awakes.

METWALI: I could murder a cup of tea. There is nothing like a cup of tea after the evening prayer. It just fills you up with warmth, makes you feel closer to God. It's chilly in here. I'll light a fire. Mind you, you'll be warm soon enough.

METWALI creates a little fire using a metal waste basket.

We need something to burn. How about your novel? I have the manuscript here. I hope you have another copy.

METWALI is holding the manuscript in his hands. He crumbles several pages and puts them in the wastebasket. He lights the fire, warms his hands against it.

Ah, who says books are useless. I liked your novel. Ms. Suzanne gave it to me to read. She said it will count as evidence against you. Are you feeling warm? Look, I'm going to remove the tape from your mouth. But if you scream it will go back on. Not that there's anyone around to hear you. Are we clear. Nod.

HISHAM nods. METWALI removes the tape.

HISHAM: Who are you?

METWALI: You can call me Metwali.

HISHAM: Metwali?

METWALI: Like the character in your novel. He was the only one I sympathised with.

HISHAM: Where is Suzanne?

METWALI: She had to leave. But don't worry I'll keep you company until she gets back.

HISHAM: What do you want from me?

METWALI: I'm what you might call a 'truth extractor', that's 'truth', not 'tooth' although I have used a drill once or twice in difficult cases.

HISHAM: You work for state security…

METWALI: How did you guess?

HISHAM: Because of your charm and good manners.

METWALI approaches closer with a pair of pliers in his hands. HISHAM thinking that METWALI is about to strike him, turns his face away.

METWALI: Don't worry you're in safe hands. No one has died under my watch. People only die when it's amateurs doing the…procedure.

HISHAM: Procedure…what procedure?

METWALI: Didn't Ms. Suzanne mention the procedure?

HISHAM: I thought she was going to give me notes on the novel.

METWALI laughs.

METWALI: Oh God you're serious. Notes on your novel? Out in the middle of nowhere. How gullible are you?

HISHAM: Does she also work for state security?

METWALI: I don't know. I don't think so. She's a bit of a mystery Ms. Suzanne.

HISHAM: Am I being held here in an official capacity?

METWALI: Stop asking so many questions. Relax. Put your trust in Allah and accept your fate. What will come will come.

Pause.

Ms. Suzanne told me something very interesting about you, she said like a lot of liberals, you are brave 'in theory'. She said you are willing to write articles criticizing the government but that you know your limits. You don't cross the red line. You keep your criticism in proportion. Because deep down, you are afraid, of the knock on the door. Of being dragged to a cell like this, tied up, made to feel absolutely helpless. This is your worst fear. So you are one of those who is brave only in theory. Who does what he can get away with but no more. Because the idea of physical pain terrifies you.

HISHAM: Listen, if it's money you want –

METWALI: How much for your freedom?

HISHAM: Just name your price. I have money.

METWALI: Would that be in your wallet?

HISHAM nods.

May I take a look?

METWALI puts his hands in HISHAM's pocket.

It's not as big as it looks from the outside.

METWALI takes out the wallet. He opens it. Counts the money.

HISHAM: I can take out more.

He removes a picture of LAYLA.

METWALI: Your wife?

Silence.

I asked you a question. Is this a picture of your wife?

HISHAM: Yes.

METWALI: She's pretty. I like a woman with full lips. Not fake. Not pumped with that crap they inject nowadays. Just natural. Where is she?

Silence.

Where is she?

HISHAM: I don't know.

METWALI: What kind of husband doesn't know where his wife is? Is she at home?

Silence.

I really hate repeating myself.

HISHAM: I don't know where she is.

METWALI looks at the photo.

METWALI: She looks feisty. Is she feisty? I bet she is out on the street, with the demonstrators. Am I right?

HISHAM: Look you can take me to the nearest ATM machine and I'll take out as much money as I can and I'll pay you and you can just let me –

METWALI: Ms. Suzanne paid me.

HISHAM: Did Suzanne ask you to do this?

METWALI: Who else.

HISHAM: So I'm not being held in an official capacity –

METWALI: You might be. I didn't enquire too deeply. Ms. Suzanne just wanted someone with my experience for the job.

HISHAM: What does she want from me? Did she tell you?

METWALI: She said she wanted a confession.

HISHAM: A confession about what? I haven't done anything.

METWALI: She told me you would say that. Mind you she needn't have bothered. Everyone says that.

HISHAM: What does she want me to confess?

METWALI: She didn't say. All she wanted from me was to loosen you up a bit.

HISHAM: Please let me go…

METWALI: Do you know what I'm going to do. I'm going to send one of my boys down to Tahrir Square to fetch your wife.

Looks at the photo

With that hair and those lips they'll soon find her. She'll feel a tap on her shoulder. She'll turn around and the boy will ask her politely: 'are you the wife of Hisham Mourad? I'm afraid he's been taken ill. You must come with me immediately'.

HISHAM: Please don't harm her.

METWALI: Oh now you are concerned. You should not have let her go on the march by herself.

HISHAM: Please…

METWALI: Over the years, I've found that is the best way to get prisoners to talk. A man can withstand physical pain. It brings out the martyr in him. But the physical pain of others, of loved ones. That's harder to bear. How long have you been married?

Pause.

HISHAM: Seven years.

METWALI: And do you still fuck her with the same intensity as when you first got married?

Pause.

I told you, I don't like repeating –

HISHAM: That's none of your damn business!

METWALI: I'm just going to go ahead and assume the answer is no. You look at her naked body, perhaps after she takes a shower and you feel nothing. You touch her and you might as well be touching your earlobe for all the desire she arouses in you. Am I right? You are ready after seven years to fuck just about anyone else other than your wife. Her flesh drains you of desire. But by bringing her here I could change all that in a matter of minutes.

HISHAM: I swear if you touch a single hair –

METWALI: You will do what? Look at yourself, you're tied to a chair in the middle of nowhere. I'm your hurricane. I'm your war. I'm your famine. Are you getting the big picture now Mr. Hisham?

HISHAM: Please you can do whatever you like to me but don't hurt Layla.

METWALI: You will thank me after I bring your wife and strip her naked in front of you. You will rediscover her body, it will be precious to you. I will tie her to a chair, legs apart and you will watch me insert my fingers into her, deep, deep into her. You will hear her gasp. And the sound of her gasp will arouse you despite yourself. You'll feel the blood pumping in your cock at the sight of me finger fucking your wife and you will feel a wonderful mix of shame and desire. And I will let you taste her.

METWALI opens HISHAM's mouth and inserts his finger into it.

And you will remember how early in your marriage you used to eat her at every opportunity like a hungry dog and you will regret that this animal desire died in you over the years. You'll be glad that I reawakened it. But tasting her is nothing compared to watching me fuck her in front of you.

HISHAM: Shut up! Shut up! Shut up!

METWALI: My balls slapping against her buttocks.

HISHAM: I'm not listening. I'm not –

METWALI claps.

METWALI: Stop screaming. Nothing has happened yet. You heard my words and played the images in your head. It's all in your imagination.

HISHAM: You fucking bastard.

METWALI: And how quickly you bought the idea that I have 'boys' under my command.

HISHAM: You total and utter fucking bastard.

METWALI: I told you. I'm just here to loosen you up a bit. Open up those closed channels in your brain. It's my job. It's what I do. And I'm good at it. Because I take pride in it. It's not my passion though. Do you want to know what my passion is? I mean besides beautiful women.

Pause.

Well I'll tell you. Pigeons. *(Pause.)* What? You look surprised. A man like me can't have such a hobby? Why not? This is what you opposition figures never appreciate. My job is stressful. Getting confessions out of people is very stressful. My hobby helps me to deal with that stress. There is nothing more relaxing after a hard day's work than to go back to my apartment block and head straight to the roof.

METWALI speaks of his pigeons with great tenderness.

I keep my pigeons in a cage that I built with these two hands. I feed them every day. Sometimes they get in a fight and they'll have wounds that need attending to. I take care of them as if they were my own children. I love those birds. I love them. I've got around twenty now and I set them free to soar high in the Cairo sky. Sometimes I imagine where they go, I'm with them, I'm flying above the noise and the pollution, above the garbage of my neighbourhood and its filthy worn down pavements, soaring so high into the air and who knows where they go, maybe as far as your neighbourhood and the apartment block you live in with your beautiful wife. You and I, we are not so different after all. We live in the same city, breathe the same air. Similar thoughts, good or bad, cross our minds. Yet there is one difference. You judge me. You give yourself the licence to judge me. I don't. I take you as you are. Tell me something, the Metwali in your novel, why does he torture the prophet even after he realises that he is a prophet, why does he do that?

HISHAM: He tortures him because he is not ready…

METWALI: Not ready for what?

HISHAM: To hear the message the prophet brings.

METWALI: I want you to know that I wouldn't do that. I would listen. I work for the state but that doesn't mean I'm happy with everything the state is doing. I'll tell you something.

Leans closer to HISHAM.

My heart is with the demonstrators. There, I said it. I don't care what son of a bitch heard it. I said it. Now that doesn't mean that if I'm asked to discipline some of them I would refuse. No, I would never neglect my duties. A job is something sacred. But if you ask me deep down what I feel, I will tell you. My heart is with the demonstrators. Tell me, is the prophet character modelled on you?

HISHAM: No.

METWALI: I didn't think so. There's something about you.

HISHAM: What?

METWALI: You are tainted somehow.

HISHAM: In what way?

METWALI: Maybe that's what we are here to find out. Your novel should be banned.

HISHAM: Why do you say that?

METWALI: Because it's blasphemous.

HISHAM: There's nothing in it against God.

METWALI: The idea of a new prophet is blasphemous. There are no prophets after the prophet Muhammad, Peace Be Upon Him. We don't live in that age, that's gone now. We live in the age of every man for himself.

HISHAM: It doesn't have to be like that.

METWALI: But that's how it is. Everyone you meet is on the make. They're only polite or courteous if you have something they want. No one has the time of day for anyone else beyond what they can get out of them.

HISHAM: You're free to do what's right. You don't have to torture people for a living. You can choose –

METWALI: Shut the fuck up. I don't need to be lectured by you. OK. Have some respect. I take pride in my work. And it's very much appreciated by my superiors and their superiors and their superiors all the way to president Mubarak himself and even beyond, all the way to the United States of America. The Americans like Egypt because we have the best interrogators on the planet. You think they give a job like that to just anyone? Here I am chatting away and time is pressing on. It's time we made some progress.

HISHAM: You don't have to do this.

METWALI: Let me look into your eyes. What's your worst fear?

He unties HISHAM's hands. HISHAM starts flailing his arms about. METWALI grabs hold of one hand and ties it to the chair's armrest. He does the same with the other hand.

It's so fucking obvious. You're a writer. You must be using those ten digits all the time. Now how does the idea of typing with no fingernails strike you?

HISHAM: Please no…

METWALI: I want you to know that you can scream as loud as you want. No one will hear you. So really go for it.

METWALI grabs a pair of pliers. Holds down HISHAM's hand and is about to extract a nail.

HISHAM: No, no, no, please stop. I'll give you all my money. Just…

METWALI: I told you, I take pride in my work.

METWALI extracts a nail from HISHAM. HISHAM screams very loudly.

One…

SCENE 3

In Tahrir Square.

LAYLA: And for a second I thought it was Hisham…

HANI: I can't believe I found you.

LAYLA: Hani.

HANI: Come on, give us a hug.

LAYLA and HANI hug.

LAYLA: You're the last person I expected to see here.

HANI: You're shivering.

LAYLA: I'm fine.

HANI: Take my coat.

LAYLA: No, honestly.

HANI: Stop being so stubborn.

HANI puts his coat around her.

LAYLA: Thanks.

HANI: I don't like watching Al Jazeera but I turned it on despite myself…I immediately thought of you, out here, all alone. No sign of Hisham?

LAYLA: He might be here. There's no way to know for certain. Sometimes I think I spot him in the crowd then I look again and it's a different face looking back at me.

HANI: He shouldn't have left you like this on your own.

LAYLA: Maybe he is finally inspired.

HANI: Still working on that novel of his.

LAYLA: Yeah.

HANI: If you were mine, I would put you ahead of everything.

LAYLA: Hani.

HANI: Have you thought some more about what I suggested?

LAYLA: What are you talking about?

HANI: The trip. To Sharm el-Sheikh.

LAYLA: You, me and Hisham going on holiday together. It's ridiculous.

HANI: Right. Then just you and me.

LAYLA: Other things have been on my mind like running away from the riot police.

HANI: You're right. I'm sorry. Maybe this is not the time to talk about a romantic getaway.

LAYLA: Maybe not.

HANI: Do you think this is it?

LAYLA: What?

HANI: The revolution. The one all you lefties have been dreaming about.

LAYLA: I hope so. Look at this crowd. I never imagined in a million years we'd have such numbers on the streets.

HANI: What do you think this will achieve?

LAYLA: Topple Mubarak.

HANI: OK, let's imagine for a moment that that happens. What difference will it really make to our lives?

LAYLA: We'll be able to breathe. We'll be free. We'll put an end to the stagnation.

HANI: It will be like the Nasser revolution of '52 all over again. The military will rule.

LAYLA: Then we keep going, protesting against them until the entire system is cleansed.

HANI: Be realistic Layla. The military will not just give up their power.

LAYLA: You're for the status quo because the system works for you. You've got your job at Vodafone so to hell with everyone else.

HANI: It's not like that.

LAYLA: I know you too well Hani.

HANI: Why do you think so badly of me?

LAYLA: You're scared, you're scared of a real change happening in this country. Which is really hypocritical. How many times have you talked to me about your time in London, how you admire their democratic system and their free press. But when it comes to Egypt, you want things to stay the same.

HANI: You can't compare us to Britain.

LAYLA: O here we go.

HANI: Democracy works only when the population is educated.

LAYLA: These are the exact same excuses the Mubarak regime churns out day in day out. 'Egypt is not ready for democracy'.

HANI: It's not.

LAYLA: That argument disgusts me. It actually makes my skin crawl. You Hani are a self-hating Egyptian –

HANI: Layla –

LAYLA: And you're a coward. I don't know what you are doing here. Just go. You don't belong in the square.

She takes off his coat and hands it to him.

HANI: I came for you –

LAYLA: I can manage by myself. Just go!

HANI: Wait just a goddamn second, will you. I mean I like it very much when you get hot and bothered, you look very sexy.

LAYLA: I said go Hani.

HANI: And seeing you fuming just makes me want to chase you on a beach like couples do in old movies.

HANI draws LAYLA closer.

And after I catch you, I'll break into song. And you'll smile and adjust my quiff.

LAYLA: Don't; people are looking.

HANI: Let them look.

LAYLA: There might be someone here who knows me.

HANI lets her go.

HANI: I just have one question. Who will win in a free and fair election?

LAYLA: That's not the point –

HANI: No, it very much is the point. You want democracy, right? Fine. Who will win in a free election? Answer me that.

LAYLA: I don't know…it will depend on the political envi –

HANI: The Muslim Brotherhood.

LAYLA: Not necessarily –

HANI: Yes, necessarily. They're the only party that has connection with ordinary Egyptians and you know it. And where will that leave us. Me a Christian Coptic and you a liberated woman who doesn't even wear the hijab?

LAYLA: Oh well, in that case let's never have democracy, let's just kiss the feet of Mubrarak and keep everything as it is –

HANI: I'm just saying the country is not ready. If we are given democracy then our future is an Islamic state.

LAYLA: Egyptians are pious but they're not stupid. Look around you, look at the youth in this crowd. They don't want to live in an Islamic republic.

HANI: But what about all the people who are not here in the square. The ones who don't have Facebook and Twitter accounts. They're the majority and they'll be easy targets for the islamists.

LAYLA: There will always be grave robbers.

HANI: What?

LAYLA: Every time I hear this argument about how Egypt is going to turn into a repressive Islamic state if it gets democracy I think about grave robbers.

HANI: That doesn't make any sense Layla.

LAYLA: In the time of the Pharaohs. A hierarchical, religious, repressive state. Right. The priests had huge powers. The Pharaohs ruled with an iron fist. They built endless palaces and temples. According to official propaganda, everyone bowed before the Pharaoh because he was seen as a God. But not everyone conformed. Certainly not the grave robbers who raided the Pharaoh's tomb. They were probably religious to the core but they were pragmatists as well and they didn't want all that gold going to waste. Egyptians are pious but they're not stupid.

Silence. LAYLA is looking ahead.

HANI: What's wrong?

LAYLA: I thought I spotted Hisham.

HANI: Are things between you still rocky?

LAYLA: Hani, look what happened between you and me, it can never be –

HANI: I just want to know. I have...I have a great deal of affection. Bollocks, that sounds lame. What I mean to say is...I care about you. O fuck it, I love you Layla.

LAYLA: Stop please.

HANI: I can't stop thinking about you.

LAYLA: Stop saying things like that.

HANI: Hisham doesn't deserve you.

LAYLA's defences are lowering.

Run away with me to Sharm.

LAYLA: I can't.

HANI: You don't have a future with Hisham. You've been married for seven years and he hasn't given you a baby. Don't you want a family?

LAYLA: Yes. But sometimes I think Hisham is right. We can't bring up a child in this country. Not as long as things remain as they are.

HANI: Wake up Layla. He's never going to change. I could give you what you want.

He puts his coat around her.

A child. A comfortable lifestyle. Security.

HANI lifts LAYLA's chin up so she is looking directly at him.

Leave Hisham and be with me. What do you say?

LAYLA contemplates HANI's offer.

SCENE 4

HISHAM is dangling from the chains attached to the ceiling. He is spread eagled. METWALI zaps him with the electrodes. HISHAM screams.

METWALI is about to zap HISHAM again when SUZANNE enters.

SUZANNE: Don't stop on my account.

METWALI zaps HISHAM again. SUZANNE sits on a chair and lights a cigarette. HISHAM mumbles some pleadings.

METWALI: What's that? Speak louder.

SUZANNE: I think he's had about enough.

METWALI: Are you sure?

SUZANNE: You can leave us alone now.

METWALI: You want me to go?

SUZANNE: Not very far. I might need you later.

METWALI: Yes Ms. Suzanne.

SUZANNE: Don't you think he's got a strange, twisted imagination.

METWALI: Yes I suppose you're right.

SUZANNE takes out a wad of cash, she waves it at METWALI. METWALI takes it and exits.

SUZANNE: There is something rather attractive about a tortured man. That's why painters couldn't get enough of Christ's wounded body. In all the museums of Europe and America, room after room of the bloodied Christ. What's behind that attraction? Guilt? Self-loathing?

HISHAM: Why?

SUZANNE: Why what?

HISHAM: Why did you do this to me?

SUZANNE: I think you will find in the end that you did this to yourself Hisham.

She takes a puff of her cigarette.

Once upon a time there were three friends. They were college friends. Hisham, Wael and Wael's girlfriend, Layla. The three friends were close. However Hisham secretly coveted Layla. He desperately wanted her for himself. But he could not compete with Wael who had charm and charisma. All three friends were politically active but it was Wael who was the real star, organizing student demos, sit-ins and writing anonymous articles that were secretly distributed. Hisham saw himself as Wael's sidekick, at best. Then one day he was approached by state security men. They took him to their headquarters in Lazoghly. They made Hisham wait for two hours before he was seen. They were probably the longest two hours of that young man's life. He knew that he could not face the idea of the physical torture that would surely follow. When they finally came for him, he was ready to confess everything he knew. And they could see that in his eyes. The information Hisham gave them about Wael exceeded the expectation of the security men. They now had good reason to target Wael because they knew for sure he was agitating against the regime. Wael was arrested, tortured, raped and crippled. They made an example of him so that other students wouldn't dare follow in his footsteps. When Wael emerged from prison, he shunned everyone he knew, including Layla. Hisham could not believe his luck when Layla confided in him and a romance began to blossom between them. No one thought that Hisham was to blame as he was Wael's best friend. And when the two friends drifted apart, everyone thought it was because of the psychological damage Wael endured. And to this day neither Wael nor Layla know of your betrayal.

Optional: SUZANNE puts out her cigarette in HISHAM's chest. Or she zaps him with the electrodes. He screams.

HISHAM: I don't know what you're talking about!

SUZANNE: It was with the help of state security that you landed your job at Al-Ahram. And your connection with them is the reason why you were never imprisoned. But that's not the worst of it. You know what disgusts me the most about you: it's only now that times are safer that you've reincarnated yourself as a writer on the left.

HISHAM: I didn't betray anyone.

SUZANNE: You destroyed his life.

HISHAM: I don't know where you got this idea from.

SUZANNE: You even modelled your prophet character on Wael. The guilt is seeping from the pages of your novel but you don't want to confront it head on. That's why you are blocked.

HISHAM: I'm innocent.

SUZANNE goes to her handbag and takes out a gun.

SUZANNE: I told you before the things we ignore have a habit of popping up later armed with sharp teeth ready to bite us. I came for your confession and I'm going to get it one way or another.

HISHAM: I didn't betray him.

SUZANNE: Lie like that one more time and it will be the last thing you say.

HISHAM: Look, it's true that state security men spoke to me but they were doing that with a lot of students.

SUZANNE: It was you who told them everything.

HISHAM: It could have been anyone –

SUZANNE: It was you. I'm going to count to ten and after that all I want to hear is your confession. One.

HISHAM: They were difficult times.

SUZANNE: Two.

HISHAM: You're right the political climate was…was…

SUZANNE: Three.

HISHAM: Much more rigid than now… We were…

SUZANNE: Four.

HISHAM: Working under difficult…

SUZANNE: Five.

HISHAM: I didn't covet Layla…

SUZANNE: Six.

HISHAM: I had no idea she would come to me…

SUZANNE: Seven.

HISHAM: I loved Wael.

SUZANNE: Eight.

HISHAM: He was my best friend.

SUZANNE: Nine. I'll fucking shoot you.

HISHAM: And, yes, I betrayed him.

SUZANNE lowers her gun, hesitates, then quickly raises it and shoots HISHAM. Brain and blood splatter against the walls.

Darkness.

SCENE 5

HISHAM and LAYLA's apartment. It is in darkness with the exception of HISHAM's laptop screen.

We hear the key in the lock. The door opens. LAYLA enters. She turns on the lights (they are soft). She spots the empty whiskey bottle on the floor. She picks it up and puts it on HISHAM's desk. She looks at the computer screen. She sits down in the chair and continues looking at the screen.

HISHAM enters from another room in the flat. He looks ghostly at first. LAYLA notices him. She gets up quickly and turns looking at HISHAM. They stare at one another for a while.

LAYLA: Do you have a cigarette? I haven't smoked the whole day.

HISHAM goes to his bookshelf and between two books, he has a cigarette pack stashed. He takes out a cigarette.

Light it for me.

HISHAM lights the cigarette then approaches closer and puts it in LAYLA's mouth. She inhales and looks away at the computer screen. HISHAM raises his hand as if he is about to stroke her hair then he lowers it.

It's blank.

HISHAM takes out a cigarette for himself and lights it.

You didn't write anything the whole day?

HISHAM sits at the edge of the table, smoking, eventually he shakes his head.

You just sat here in the darkness staring at a blank computer screen?

HISHAM: No.

LAYLA: You wrote something.

HISHAM: No. I didn't sit staring at the blank screen.

LAYLA: What did you do then?

HISHAM: Sometimes I stared out of the window.

LAYLA: At what?

HISHAM: Pigeons mostly. I thought a fair bit about pigeons today.

LAYLA: Is that supposed to be some kind of joke.

HISHAM: No.

LAYLA: How did it go?

HISHAM: How did what go?

LAYLA: Your meeting with Suzanne.

HISHAM: It didn't happen.

LAYLA: Why not?

HISHAM: She called to cancel.

LAYLA: But the phones were down.

HISHAM: She called on the landline.

LAYLA: Did she give a reason for cancelling?

HISHAM: She said she was going down to Tahrir Square.

LAYLA: I knew it!

HISHAM: You knew what?

LAYLA: I thought I saw her today. I couldn't be sure.

HISHAM: In Tahrir?

LAYLA: Yes. She was with Wael.

HISHAM: That makes sense.

LAYLA: Does it?

HISHAM: They're lovers.

LAYLA: How do you know?

HISHAM: She told us, at the British Council dinner.

LAYLA: I don't remember.

HISHAM: Maybe you were talking to someone else when she mentioned it.

LAYLA: Why did she tell you that?

HISHAM: What do you mean?

LAYLA: How did the subject come up in conversation? Did you ask her if she was seeing someone?

HISHAM: No.

LAYLA: Then what? She just blurted it out. 'By the way, I'm fucking Wael Said'.

HISHAM: Yea, more or less. Do you want a drink?

LAYLA: Hisham!

HISHAM: She knew about our history. Our days at the university. I guess Wael told her. I'm fixing a drink. Do you want one?

LAYLA: You finished the Glengoyne.

HISHAM: There wasn't much left in the bottle.

LAYLA: It's a shitty habit, drinking as you write.

HISHAM: I don't do it every day.

LAYLA: You really didn't write anything today?

HISHAM: No. But I made some progress. Layla there is something…

LAYLA: What?

HISHAM: Let's have a drink first. I'll fetch some ice.

LAYLA: I don't want a drink. I need to talk to you too.

HISHAM: Yes?

LAYLA: I've reached a decision.

HISHAM: It sounds ominous. Is it ominous?

LAYLA: Maybe you better fetch the ice first.

> *HISHAM heads to the kitchen. LAYLA takes off HANI's coat. HISHAM comes back from the kitchen with a glass, an ice tray and a whiskey glass. He puts the ice and the glass on the desk then heads to the drinks cupboard under the bookshelves. Opens it, searches through the bottles.*

HISHAM: Vodka, Vodka, Arak, Rum, this is not looking good, Ah, Whiskey. Panic over.

> *He pours the whiskey in the glass. Puts a few ice cubes.*

LAYLA: You normally drink it neat.

HISHAM: The ice will slow me down. You're sure you don't want one?

> *LAYLA shakes her head.*

Did you talk to him?

LAYLA: Who?

HISHAM: Wael.

LAYLA: No.

HISHAM: Why not?

LAYLA: He was up on a platform. They had erected this platform and that's when I saw Suzanne pushing him up the ramp.

HISHAM: Did he speak?

LAYLA: He tried to. Someone handed him a megaphone. It wasn't working. I could barely make out what he was saying.

HISHAM: He was always a brilliant orator.

LAYLA: At first I was angry that the megaphone wasn't working. I really wanted to hear him. But then I thought it didn't matter. Today is not about one man leading us out of the darkness. Somehow that idea seems to belong to another age.

HISHAM: Still, it would have been good to hear him. He sacrificed so much for this country.

LAYLA: But this is not about figureheads. We don't need them.

HISHAM: How did he look?

LAYLA: What do you mean?

HISHAM: Has he aged?

LAYLA: He was too far. I couldn't make out his features.

HISHAM: He used to give out a kind of light when he spoke.

LAYLA: I think you revered him far too much.

HISHAM: Layla I…

LAYLA: What?

HISHAM takes a gulp of whiskey.

HISHAM: Nothing. You know I sat here all day thinking about all sorts of things. I was afraid for you. I had terrible guilt about letting you go out on your own.

LAYLA: As you should.

HISHAM: I imagined you being kidnapped from the street. All sorts of terrible and dark thoughts came into my head.

LAYLA: Hey, it's OK.

HISHAM: I have this terrible feeling of guilt. It sits like a stone over my heart –

LAYLA: It's alright Hisham. I was alright. Yes I would have liked you to have been with me. But I was fine on my own –

HISHAM: That's not what I meant –

HISHAM is about to confess everything when LAYLA interrupts him.

LAYLA: Listen. This was the beautiful thing about today.
Egyptians from all backgrounds came together. The rich
and the poor came together and for the first time in my
life I saw that that is possible. It wasn't just some stupid
leftist dream. It happened today. We were together. The
poor looked after the rich and we owe it to them to see
this revolution all the way through. Not just till Mubarak
is toppled and his henchmen are behind bars, not just till
we have free elections and a foreign policy that is truly
our own. No, the goal should be to improve their lives.
To lift them out of their poverty. That will be the mark
of our success. The chant today was 'bread, freedom,
social justice' In that order, starting with bread. Hisham, I
reached a decision.

HISHAM: Layla, I have to tell you something –

LAYLA: Wait, I've got to get this off my chest first. Just now,
before I came back, I was with Hani. I bumped into him in
Tahrir Square. Actually he came specially to find me. Hani
and I…I never told you this before but Hani kissed me at
Dalia's Christmas party.

HISHAM: What?

LAYLA: I'm sorry Hisham –

HISHAM: I've always hated that guy. How could you have
kissed him?

LAYLA: He tried to persuade me to run off to Sharm el-Sheikh
with him. I'll be lying if I said I wasn't tempted.

HISHAM: You love him?

LAYLA: No, you have to believe me. I don't. I love you. But we
can't go on as we have been.

HISHAM: What do you mean?

LAYLA: You haven't touched me in three months!

HISHAM: And that's reason to run off with Hani!

LAYLA: I told you I'm not running away with him. I came back
tonight didn't I? But would you have noticed if I hadn't?

HISHAM: Of course I would. I was worried sick about you.

LAYLA: You would carry on staring out of the window, thinking about pigeons. Do you love me Hisham? Do you even want to be with me anymore?

HISHAM: I do.

LAYLA: Then you will hear the decision I've reached.

HISHAM: How could you have kissed him?

LAYLA: Will you stop thinking about that.

HISHAM: You drop a bombshell on me like that and you don't expect me to react.

LAYLA: It was just a kiss/

HISHAM: Oh, I should be grateful it wasn't just a fuck/

LAYLA: Not even a good kiss/

HISHAM: How could you?

LAYLA: I don't remember much about it. I was drunk. I was vulnerable. Do you have any idea how self-absorbed you have been. We are stuck. Our marriage is like a car trapped in mud.

HISHAM: You want to leave me?

LAYLA: I've thought about it.

The sound of people chanting outside.

What's going on?

They both head to the window.

HISHAM: It's a march.

LAYLA: People coming back from Tahrir. We should go and join them.

HISHAM: Now?

LAYLA: Why not? You've sat here all day whilst the revolution took place and now the revolution is coming right up to your window. What are you waiting for?

HISHAM: OK but first tell me what decision you have reached.

LAYLA: Can I have a sip?

HISHAM hands LAYLA the whiskey. She takes a gulp.

We are going to have a baby.

HISHAM: You're pregnant!

LAYLA: No. I mean I will stop the contraception and we will go ahead and have a baby. It is time. And if you refuse Hisham then we can't stay together. This is the decision I reached. What do you say?

HISHAM downs the rest of the whiskey. Optional: In another part of the stage WAEL in his wheelchair and SUZANNE appear (as earlier in Act 2 scene 1).

All these years I've been afraid. I didn't want to bring a baby into this country with all of its corruption and chaos but after what I've seen today, what ordinary people can do if they band together, it has restored my faith in humanity.

Optional: Slowly SUZANNE turns her head to look at at HISHAM. Their eyes meet.

HISHAM: Layla, I have –

LAYLA: And I know a year from now, two years, the situation might turn for the worst. It's not going to be easy.

HISHAM: I have –

LAYLA: But still that doesn't take away from the beauty and the bravery and the defiance we showed today. The power of all of us that I felt surging through my body. There will never be a better time to bring a child into the world/

HISHAM: I have something to tell you.

Darkness.

The End.

BY THE SAME AUTHOR

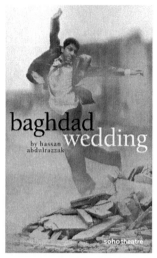

Baghdad Wedding
9781840027839

'In Iraq, a wedding is not a wedding unless shots get fired. It's like in England where a wedding is not a wedding unless someone pukes or tries to fuck one of the bridesmaids. That's the way it goes.'

From cosmopolitan London to the chaos of war-ravaged Baghdad, this is the comic tale of three friends, torn between two worlds, and a wedding that goes horribly wrong.

Baghdad Wedding premiered at the Soho Theatre in June 2007.

WWW.OBERONBOOKS.COM

 Follow us on www.twitter.com/@oberonbooks
& www.facebook.com/oberonbook